i

All I Want Is Peace

Sarah Condor-Fisher

All I Want Is Peace

Copyright ©2020 by Sarah P. Condor-Fisher

6.0" x 9.0" (15.24 x 22.86 cm)

Black on White paper

113 pages

ISBN-13: 9798554491405

Imprint: Independently published

Library of Congress Publication Data

      Condor-Fisher, Sarah, P. (1972-   )

Genre: Nonfiction – Poetry – American – General

      Date of first publication: 2020

TX 8-908-411

Printed in the United States of America

Contents:

All I Want Is Peace

Something Beautiful Has Died

Something beautiful has died

The world has lost a gem

An ever-blooming flower

A blossoming tree

A bluebird fell from the sky

A hummingbird was drowned

A butterfly got caught

In Black Widow's web

Something beautiful has died

Yet no-one really cares

The world goes on and on

Merciless and cold!

The world is a poorer place

Where only wealth remains

Greed, envy, jealousy...

Something beautiful has died

And only I despair.

Years Ago

Years ago, I would wait in the wings of the dusk

For the Queen of the Night to appear

And guide my steps along the streets

Winding like snakes around the houses and parks

Slumbering in soft repose, not even I

Part ghost, part passenger from another planet

Could rouse them to converse

All was silent, yet it spoke to me

In words of thousands of feet and faces

That could not see what I could see

Breathing the same air, inhabiting the same space

All things have a soul, and shame on us

If we fail to listen, fail to hear, fail to see

But I could see more than I desired

I was invisible once, tagging along shadows

Through shadowless nights, dark corners and empty

benches

I saw the worst places, things and acts

I slept where my feet grew tired

Under bridges, alcoves, in the street...

I liked it that way, for I was free – and yet

Not quite free, living without

Within, an empty shell

Filled with Otherness of things around

For Freedom to exist, there must be a not-free place

Like your body, your house, things that tie you down

I had no such place

I was no such body

Yet, there was magic in those nights

When the Queen took me by the hand

And showed me the secrets of Beyond

Aye, even the quiescence of Death

Though it was years before I met Him face-to-face

Longing for ultimate Freedom, knowing

It is Nothingness

Wishing for ultimate Feeling, growing

Numbed to pain

All things have a soul, and you speak to them

And when you listen, you will hear them speak

They tell you secrets of thousands of men

Humans that walked around as you do

Had the same thoughts, felt the same pain

And desperately sought for answers

In the morning cup of tea, with the world out-of-focus

Mechanically following the routine of the day

The mechanics of Existence

Until the late-night cigarette and a final thought

That there is nothing Beyond

A deep thought, all permeating thought, a thought without

substance

Finally rejoicing in the safe harbor right here

By the bed, on the couch, in the bedroom

Among most familiar things, things that need no souls

Because they are you...

What are you without them?

That was my thought as I woke up in the rain on a bench

by the gas station

Me

What is Me?

A congregation of atoms, molecules, carbons from a

distant star

Hydrogen from the Big Bang, oxygen from the weed under

my feet

I grew without knowing

I knew without growing

Yet, My Substance is adding up to more than dust from all

the stars

I shine with a thousand lights, much more today than

years ago

When the Queen of the Night held my hand

To show me the ultimate Darkness

I shine because She was there for me then.

Now, she is there for You. Stay silent, listen, absolve

yourself

Be patient and suffer through

One day soon, you too will smile and shine.

In the Shade of My Greenwood Tree

In the shade of my greenwood tree

I shall repose, and patiently

Wait for the guidance from the Lord

No earthly praises, no award

Only my angel in the sky

A squirrel, rose, the tree, and I

For none can harm the one who seeks

Rewards in sunshine, mountain peeks

No ill can come to one who yearns

Beyond world's pleasures and returns

Beyond the blight of envy, greed

And struggle for your bread and breed

My fights are done, my battles won

A new Path for me has begun

I no more fight and will not flee

For I am where I want to be

In the shade of my greenwood tree.

Thinking of Love

Do you think of love

The way I do – alone, in the dark, filled with longing

Memories peeking from under the desk,

Little sweethearts strolling to the bathroom and back

The floor kissed by those cherished feet, now gone,

The air filled with that warm, joyous breath

Photographs on hinges, taped on the drawing door

Smiling at you from Beyond by the kitchen sink –

And then you go out and see

Loneliness – that you never saw before:

A deserted woman eating a takeaway lunch on a park

bench

Plastic bags, cups, Tupperware...

Plastic thoughts about plastic people living in a plastic

world

Water in plastic bottles, stirring coffee with a plastic spoon

Even cars are neatly painted to look like steel

Can love survive in this plastic world?

Then there are lonely men who lock the doors behind

To drink in peace, to watch TV, to forget –

Not speaking unless spoken to

Not thinking unless thought of –

And there is no-one to think of them:

Children, grandchildren, step-this and that – all gone

All have their lives

All have their loves

Transporting them in plastic cars, feeding them with

plastic spoons

Cherishing them – with plastic thoughts?

I should hope not.

But then again, here I am, in the middle of the night

Thinking of Love

Surrounded by Love – and yet

Alone

Life is too long to suffer even one Great Loss

Life is too short to cherish even one Great Gain

And so we move on, somewhere in-between

Tasting, smelling, feeling the memories, mementoes,

artifacts...

At least they have no plastic aftertaste

Though we have been there before

And emerged wiser for having had the experience

Stronger for having loved

Braver for having lost what we cherished the most.

For Every Joy We Have to Pay

For every joy in life we have to pay

For every smile and kiss and caring word

There will come sorrows which won't go away

The shield is useless – if you don't have the sword

To live alone in peace is not enough

To have all joy from sunshine, birds and flowers

You'll long for more, your unrequited love

Will stab your Heart and minutes seem like hours

You'll think of the past, castles in the sand

The blue from the sky of your childhood dreams

A caring word, a soft and loving hand

Sheltered from the world, its cold, cruel schemes

But now there's no shelter, no peace will last

Great Happiness and Love? They pass away

And you but weep, for living in the past

Is not an option, and not your role to play

You are too human, and must face the pain

Though from it all you sometimes wish to flee

To leave, the world to never see again

To give up, surrender to destiny –

But there's so much that on your choice depends

Your pets and flowers, your duty to the past

And though you may think that you have no friends

There's love out there – 'tis waiting, till the last!

So though for joys in life we have to pay

The Beauty which we share is worth that price

Blossoming trees will line our rocky way

Treasures of Life are worth the sacrifice

Butterfly

There's anemone by the nutmeg tree

Sages and lupines, a wild berry bush

I stroll there every morning, look for thee

And meet a butterfly, with wings so lush

A queen would envy him that silken robe

With joyful pride he hovers in the air

Selects the sweetest of petals to probe

And glances my way, the moment to share

I must rejoice to see You – painless, free…

My minutes turn to days, and days to weeks

Cuddles looks up and starts to comfort me

He knows too well why tears roll down my cheeks.

What Is Life?

What is this life but hours and days

Of sleep and work, some rest, some praise

And all the years add up to few

Moments, seconds that we knew

Would carry us through all the rest –

Dire struggles, battles, trials, tests...

We'd always have that Flame within

That warmed us, warned us from the Sin

Of taking for granted what we have

And scorning Life and taunting Death

For, in the end, what else remains

After all the wars and pains?

Nothing – but those precious minutes

We recall when all is finished

They all add up to – weeks, perhaps

If we've been lucky, loved and blessed

Seventy years boils down to days

A post-card with that three-word phrase.

All I Want Is Peace

I want but peace, and all I have is war

I pet my past, yet past is all but gone

I sail wide seas, but crave my narrow shore

I wish to pause, but my Will spurs me on

I've lived through Pain that few have felt or known

I've loved with Love that none could comprehend

I've been to places none dare go alone

And, in that Darkness, found my truest Friend

It's with a happy eye that I look back

Upon my convoluted crisscross trip

I suffered, starved, but never did I lack

In helpful winds and blessings for my Ship

I weathered storms and battles, won the War

I held the Chalice, touched the Golden Fleece

You name it, my friend – I've been there before

And now, I'm done – and all I want is Peace.

The Country of Desire

There is a river gently flows

Through the Country of Desire

There is a place that no-one knows

Where we'll build our tent and fire

There we will sleep and watch the skies

You will hold and squeeze my hand

For us the stars and Moon will rise

And our love will never end

It is our country and our stream

We have been there both before

Alone, together, in a dream

Now, we return, forevermore.

Struggle

The bird is turning, twisting, raving

The bird is in attack

There is no knowing how it's ending

There is no going back!

The sky is heavy, grim and falling

Closing in on the bird

The day is dark with dust appalling

Up is down – how absurd!

The sun is struggling, seething, hissing

All noises of the Earth

Are merging, aiming at, missing

The bird, the bird, the bird!

And Gods are grinning, giggling, jesting

Watching the scene they stirred

Watching me down as I am praying –

For my Heart, for the bird.

The Knight and His Lady

The Knight gets up, prepares his horse

His lady still asleep

He has a duty, sets the course

With promises to keep

At early sunrise, he sails out

While she remains behind

His lady, his home, his redoubt

His heart and soul and mind

The day is long, he spurs his horse

And pauses for a drink

His blood is Viking, Celtic, Norse

His Heart is starry brink

His lady guards his treasured home

With Love and Faith and Trust

With Love she's never all alone

Two hearts – a sacred truss!

The Knight comes home and feeds his horse

Then rushes for a kiss

The strongest of all is the Force

That all day he has missed

The Lady smiles and says those words

For which he fought and killed

And then like two small loving birds

They cherish what they built.

I Live to Remember

It's like "cat love" I heard her say
In a most scornful, scolding way
She sipped of wine and drowned her pain
She said she'd never love again

She lived on dirt-cheap cigarettes
Filled with self-pity and regrets
An empty table, glass of wine
That was her only Valentine

And I felt sorry for her then
Thinking about her past, the men
That paved her road to solitude
And made this lady cold and crude

Hard work and wine was all she had
Recalling childhood, always sad
Like some are wont to bring the days
Before the Flood and Homer's lays

When men were angels, pure and free

And Paradise our destiny...

Then came the Fall, with war and blight

Spirit turned ghost, and ghost a sprite...

All that took place so long ago

But for my mom I would not know

Painted in smoke on whitewashed walls

Her voice still rises – and then falls

Into the visage of my youth...

I don't need smoke and drink to sooth

The Love I fell in, was no trap

My sweetheart cat purrs in my lap

I kiss my Beloved's photograph

And live to remember – to love and laugh.

The Power of Love

Such is the power of love in me

That it can alter destiny

That it can unfreeze hearts of ice

Unlock the gates of Paradise

And it can turn despair to joy

And make a man from any boy!

I've seen it happen times and times

I can describe it in my rhymes

And stranger things have happened yet –

Through the love of a dog and cat

I have been altered deep within

And purified of every sin!

There's magic great in love we wield

Stronger by far than sword and shield

Love is the magic in all respects

In every form and kind and sex

And if you slight it and deny

Desperate, lonely, you will die.

I Am Become a Name

"I am become a name," they'll say

Using my words from here and now

A hundred years hence, perhaps more

They'll pause to wonder at my lore

And what I spoke and why and how

Wherefore I lived my life each day:

Was it in pleasure, pain, or play?

In the Sun? The shade of a bough?

And what lies or lay at the core

Of lines that none has heard before

Lines which are simple and low-brow

Yet secrets within may betray...

But I will have no secrets then

I will have spoken all to all

Made strong by Time and Fate and Love

I will have given just enough

To please, allure, but not appall

With easy strokes of my pure pen

"I am become a name," again

The line dissolves, the name grows small

A brave bird pauses on the bluff

For life is made from subtle stuff –

The feather, flight, the Heart and Soul

Dreams and hopes that cloak a name

Unique, and yet so much the same

    As yours.

Love

Love is a self-substantial fuel

Which owns thee without being owned

Love is tenderness that's cruel

Future which cannot be postponed

Being in love is being good

For love will give and ask for none

The one who loves, does as he should

It is through Love God's Will is done

Love asks no reasons, sets no goals

Love is the Reason and the Goal

Love shuns the master who controls

And scorns the slave who sold his soul

Love is my sole resolve and creed

Love is all I will ever need.

The Storm

Thirty years now I've trodden through the land
Of bristled bushes and wild, waspish trees
That try to trip me, forbiddingly bend
Above my head – and push me to my knees

I pray: What monsters out there walk the earth
Lying in wait, in shadows all around
Whatever evils cruel gods gave birth
I pray for Peace and Love, without a sound

For I fear the storm – feel it – it arrives
Cold winds whip and flay, sharp sleet hits my eyes
I flee, I drop, I wish to die at times…
I swear, I weep – but no-one hears my cries

I crave for peace, a stable place, soft soil
That does not move and answers to a Flower
The skies grow darker, they simmer and boil
Each treacherous second feels like an hour

Ominous branches are flogging the air

Spearing each other, like swords without shields

Monsters of legends, horror everywhere!

I drop and watch that fight – then something yields

For I can see it's not me they attack

I am but a meek human passing through

And once I pass, I won't be coming back...

I smile – the monsters do not have a clue!

The elemental minds, the jungle fight

The picture that the gods have granted me

Is here to distill my day through the night

To usher in my Dream – not Destiny!

Though I'm but a speck of dirt from a star

No warrior, no hero by any means

Yet, I have been through hell, and come this far

After this tempest, all will ease, it seems

It's through me that the picture means a thing

I am the thing that means, and without me

The storm, the trees, the fighters in the ring

Would crumble, shrivel, rot, and cease to be.

All She Knows of Death and Life

I watch her cross the street each night

On softest tiptoes, like a ghost

Her shadow lingers in my sight

She's a ship in search for a coast

She is a bird without a nest

Flying, unseen, in the Beyond

A spirit tired that seeks to rest

A Nature's child in winter spawned

She is a mood, a passing whim

A grace of God uncaptured yet

With hungry eyes and future grim

She sometimes wishes she were dead

But all she knows of death and life

Is lie in wait and kill a rat

Is darkness, struggle, endless strife

At times too much for a small cat...

Open Your Heart

What is it I look for?

What is it I adore?

The things I've always sought:

Laughter with pain unwrought

Happiness, Joy profound

That few have ever found

Peace of the standstill sea

Natural harmony –

Calm breeze upon my face

Blessings at every place...

All I perceive, my Soul

Always joyful and whole

The world always as One

The trees, the birds, the Sun

Even though I am gone

These lines stay here to please

With happiness and peace

With a prayer for You

The friend I never knew...

Soft ye now, not a sound

My Soul is still around

The places I have been

Creatures I've met or seen...

What makes You cannot die!

Ponder it when you lie

At home, alone, in bed

Your thoughts blue, your eyes red

And yellow in the gut?

I've been there too, I shut

That door and built that wall

Out of fear, feeling small

And helpless, all alone...

Yes, all your aches I've known

And more! Then, took it down

Brick by brick, line by line

And sought a lucky sign

An "omen" if you will

I listened, I stood still

Allowed my Soul to rise

With bluebirds, butterflies:

Suck on the nectar sweet

Petals with kisses greet!

All I had ever sought

Instantly was brought

Within my reach, my Friend!

Open your Heart and hand!

For all that You adore

Is for You here – and more!

She Weeps for Him

She weeps for him, for he is dead

But yesterday, he walked this Earth

Was born the thorny road to tread

And fought and loved from birth

Like Aeneas, like Odysseus

He set a steady course to sail

He won no fleece, no golden goose

He was no Fuhrer you would hail

He was an "ordinary man"

Yet so special, so filled with Grace

Part General, part Peter Pan

A twinkling eye, a smiling face...

She weeps for him, for Joy has died

Her memories her sorrow feed

She has been gutted, torn inside

It's tears and moans her heart does bleed!

Lost echoes of his voice at dawn

Reverberate with chill in air

Alone, alone she struggles on

He's gone – and yet is everywhere!

At night, she strolls outside to scream

To kill the pain, to quench the char

And lifts her head as in a dream

She sees him twinkling on a star

His twitching nose, his warm bright eyes

She reads the message in the skies:

My Love, I'm here. Please, do not cry.

My Love, for you, I'll never die!

Rainbows

Have you seen rainbows, bright and clear?

Have you felt the desire

To cross beneath, to come so near

So as to touch that fire?

Maybe cold, a vision perhaps

But still a fire divine

Which with your touch could collapse

Or with your breath untwine...

It's after rain that they appear

After the storm has passed

A sign from God you need not fear

Of Beauty unsurpassed

I cheat at times, I must confess

I make my very own

With a garden hose I compress

To make a water cone

Over the grass and trees and flowers

A bluebird: "You! You! You!"

My friend, he doesn't like the showers

Though he loves rainbows too

Every morning, he looks at me

We marvel at the sight

I make a wish, then carefully

Turn off the water-spout

Forgive me God, but there are not

Rainbows enough to sprout

All wishes and dreams in the world

All Beauty, Faith, and Love.

My Hibiscus

There's my Hibiscus in his peak

Next to the sunflowers I planted

Each morning and evening we speak

I'm all abashed and enchanted

Roses are listening, two steps back

For there is something about him

That the beautiful roses lack –

A spirit of pride, prime and prim

Like a warrior, he stands alone

Pines to the Sun, craves for love

An untraveled hero, unknown

To the world – but not God above

He is like you, giving joy

Even in rain, on a dull day

Petals for eyes, he's quite a boy

As tall and bright as you, I say!

And when we speak, I sense you're there

Answering my pleas, soothing pain

And I touch you, with utmost care

And then we are one, once again.

Nothing to Erase

Would I want to know the future?

Would I want to erase the past?

Then, what would I do – start again?

Through this convoluted journey

This maze of mirrors we call Life

With stops and starts, rises and falls?

Out of the darkness, Sirens call

Temptations, thrills and frills of days

Curious suitors – coming, going

Passing by the window at dusk...

Go! Go! I don't mind lonely dawns

Though I fade at times, like a flower

Plucked yesterday, starved for the Sun

The Sun I had known as a child –

Isn't it the same Sun, the same I?

Why erase yesterday? Why mourn

For what has been, with eager eyes

Pointing to the horizon now...

Now is the Future and the Past –

There is nothing beyond, nothing

      To erase.

Let Us Be Brave

Let us be brave

All problems resolve

With ultimate Faith

And virulent verve

Let us be brave

And never lose nerve

For good man or knave

For all that we serve

Let us be brave

For we simply must

Inspire with Faith

Hope, Love, and Trust.

My Last Line

I'm done today...
I'm wont to say
With the last line
Comma and word

Period dropped
In the dark room –
Wine, beer, and jest...
Now let me swoon

You got the gist
You read my verse
You have my trust
Prolix yet terse

Midnight is past
I am still here
But I won't last
That much is clear

I'm done today

No more to say

'tis my last line

Period. Done.

Now, I am gone.

What Does Not Kill Me Will Make Me Stronger

Even small pain may be beyond bearing

The inner pain, the fight within, tearing

Your Soul and Heart apart, because of life

Which has demands, and cuts you with a knife

You cannot see it, you can feel the stabs

They nail you to the wall, pound you with jabs

And when you can't take it any longer

Think: "What doesn't kill me, will make me stronger…"

But how strong should you be, or can you be?

And what kind of strength is this? Fight or flee

Is not an option they will let you take –

Yet, they too, in darkest hours, caught a break

For none of us can make it on our own

All alone, no friends, in the dark a-groan…

You'll get killed that way, you know it full-well

Listen to what fairy tales have to tell

About the monsters of the forests deep:

You roam alone, without a friend or sleep

Looking out for omens on every tree –

This is about your Will, not Destiny!

And, shall I say, I have been there before

Fumbling and floundering, feet worn and sore

Struggling through darkness deep without an end

Longing for help, begging God for His hand

Pausing and pondering, plucking petals

To answer my yes-or-no, where-to-go…

Questions like you have now – no-one will know

The answer better than you! Don't wander!

Make up your mind, and go! Never look back!

They can't kill you – only you can do that

For you are as strong as you need to be

To walk the path you've chosen: Destiny

Is just a word for those who lack the Will

It is by doing you will learn the skill

To overcome, get up, and fight again

To revel in fighting, cherish the pain

To tell yourself, when you can't bear it any longer:

"What does not kill me will make me stronger!"

Let's Conquer Joy

In deep regrets we all have toiled —

Songs we sing, photographs we clutch…

With searing pain we can't avoid

That tears our eye and numbs our touch

In the most beautiful of songs

Excruciating sadness lies

Someone for someone always longs

And someone somewhere always cries

All we can do is try to gain

Control by Will, release the Heart

Convert to Pleasure all our pain

With Courage turn to God and Art

Let's start again, ourselves forgive

Redress with Hope what ills have passed —

There is no other way to live

Than here and now, not in the past

Not to revive the blame and pain

Not in the future, in our dreams

To scorn the present in that vein

And feel our Hearts burst in the seams...

Let's grasp the moment to extreme

Let's conquer Joy and never vane

Let us be stronger than we seem

In God, in Love – and in our Pain!

How Do I Love Thee

How do I love Thee? You have never asked

And, if you asked, what would I tell?

Love is a sacred charm, a spell

Which may be crushed as fast as it was cast

How do I love Thee? I could not express

The depths of oceans, heights of skies

The pleasures of our Paradise

The Trust and Faith and Joy which I possess

When I think of you, and feel you within

When I touch your hair, kiss your eyes

When I hear your voice, kind and wise

Advise me to beware of lies and sin...

How do I love Thee? Far beyond this life

My Love spans to the Moon and Sun

You'll feel it on the rays to run

Straight through your pupils to your Heart, my Love

Will never end and we will never part.

An Unhallowed Bliss

How can I beat the Beauty of the rose?

How can I equal sunflower's warmth and joy?

Or vie with trees in autumn leafy clothes?

What words or imagery can I employ?

I fear old Plato may have had a point

I paint in words, but what a feeble tongue

Compared to the gems God did here anoint

Birdie's chirp, not mine, is the divine song!

My life is vain, my art a poorer try

To equal God's in grace and majesty

A miserable greedy wretch am I

Reaching to grasp His brilliance in me!

Yet, I too am God's creature, am I not?

Aren't I made in His image, here to bless

The world with Beauty? I partake of God

And point out the pearls that others miss

Here is a line for you, sealed with a kiss

To remember me, now that I am gone:

Rejoice! Your life is an unhallowed bliss!

Do what I did: Go, bring the joyful Sun

From around, from within – to everyone!

Mission San Juan Capistrano

There's a stone house, parched by the Sun

Many secrets it shrouds within

Built the year this country was won

As a refuge from earthly sin

There is no priest – once, there was one

Converts and natives lived here then

And refuge-seekers, on the run

Hispanic, White, and Indian

Leveled, rebuilt in eighteen-twelve

Its columns still stand, roof gives shade

Enter and you will find God dwells

In the small chapel, simply made

Stone walls, plain candles, hard-wood pews

And an ornate alter of gold!

With silence and peace to transfuse

With Jesus and Love to behold

Swallows come to nest here each year

Next to the bells that rarely peal

But remain, for the atmosphere,

For the penitent's heart to heal

To heal at the sight of the past

In the world of silence and peace

To light a candle, pray at last

For the Loved One who is not here

Pray to God at the altarpiece

Pray to forgive, and shed a tear.

Philosopher

In a warn suit without a tie

He sits and muses at his desk

He thinks thoughts no money can buy

He strikes a pose quite statuesque

He thinks he is, therefore he thinks

But he thinks that therefore he is

After the pipe, after the drinks

He thinks not thinking is a bliss –

But can he exist and not think?

Can he absolve himself of thought?

There are more thoughts than there is ink

Yet thinking is not what he sought...

He sought the reason for living

He sought the truth, happiness, love

How to find taking in giving

To pass through the needle above

He sought – something. He forgot what

Meanwhile his thought became his Self...

Now he's gone, I peruse his thought

I muse and wonder, pray to God

Then I put him back on the shelf

For I have found all that I sought.

The Puppet Generation

Enraged, enflamed – something is happening
Outside, in the dark: "It will be our night!
Put the mask on, bro, and let's go! Let's go!"
The International they proudly sing
And tell themselves their future is all bright
"It's Lenin, Che, Mao, Marx Two Point Oh!"

But, oh, poor sheep! How little do they know!
Offals of the past barely out of sight
Misled and fed on lies, now want to sink
Columbia, drown her in Doublethink!
Cowards, with covered faces, through the night
Where are you marching? Where you want to go?

Sadness fills the poet at such a sight
So many young souls chained up, without Grace
The Puppet Master's old, distorted face
Smiles, pulls the strings – and they follow, and smite!

Where the one-eyed lead the blind, blindness rules
Extolling errors of the past – what fools!

Why, You Funny!

Why – you have such funny long paws!
You naked, you bare, you so big!
Your ears are flat, instead your nose
Sticks out of your face like a rig!

The toes you touch me with feel nice
It's chewy, what you call it? Hand?
Why, you never look out for mice?
And catch no birds? Even when you stand!

Your head is big and round, with fur
Which curls and falls on your face!
When we cuddle, why don't you purr?
And why always sit at my place?!

Come, my dear, stop playing all day
Though I am not perfect, like you
God knew why He made us this way
Though you and I don't have a clue

And does it matter anyway?

I love you more than words can say!

When All My Days Have Passed

So much is left to do...

So little time

I mourn the days of youth

Wasted in play

Pointless walks, wasteful talks

Playing all day...

But isn't it play

That life is all about?

Romp and tussle:

Lions learn to kill in play

Children, to love...

Cease to play, cease to live!

When all my days have passed

Before I go

The final hour will be

A playful show

Of what it was about

A memory

Of sunsets, starry skies

Kisses in rain

Rose petals on my lips

All love, no pain

Touchés and funny slips

And friends, again

Who had helped me out in need

Foes, without whom

You wouldn't read these lines

They made me strong

Fight, survive, and conquer

Protect and love

I'll look back on my life

Content and proud

With one regret, but one:

I could have given love

Where I saw none

I could have given more –

Then, I will pardon all

Even myself.

I Rise to Fight Again

I am kicked about, slapped and smashed
Pounded by fists, knocked to my knees
They are waiting for me to crash
They want me to beg, say "Stop, please..."

They grab me by the neck and squeeze
Dollar signs for eyes, they want cash!
They want my Love and memories –
Or else, they'll turn me into ash!

But with each kick I grow in strength
Each kick and blow brings me less pain
I smile within, peace comes at length
I know how to dance in the rain!

I rise and see them from above
They are all cowards, weaklings, trash!
I laugh! I wield the Power of Love!
My Soul, my Heart, they cannot smash!

I rise and see them grow insane

They twist and squirm in pools of sleaze

And, as I rise to fight again,

I see them frozen, white as cheese!

For hate and greed consume their own

You always reap what you have sown.

There Is Not Much to Life

There is not much to life:

A touch, a kiss, gentle caress

A moment in the Sun

A sniff-and-wiggle of the tail

A gentle purr perhaps

A coo-coo of a dove outside

Afternoon breeze, a stroll

Your favorite song on your lips

Without expectations

Grateful for every moment here

Even those which are gone

Especially those which are gone

Because, somehow, you know

Listening to the hum of the world

Being for the moment

By the strangest of ironies

Is what Forever means

There is not much to life –

Your Forever is now.

A Connoisseur of Love

I am a connoisseur of Love

I come from nowhere, I'm just passing by, watching

Observing the grass grow and people speak

Sitting in circles outside, assuring each other

That they are safe, that the world is safe, that Life

Is something they *have* and can believe in

Much like birds believe in solid nests

And cats in unseen hideaways

And dogs in whatever the master says is good

Because they love us –

Love is everywhere and yet

We seem to rarely grasp it, always filled with doubt…

We could swim in oceans of love, but we fear

Drowning, the depths below, the bottom we can't see,

Side waves, the unknown, unfamiliar, water up the nose…

Love is everywhere and yet

We can never satisfy our *need*, we never get enough…

Do birds get depressed for lack of love?

Do roses fade away and die for lack of a kiss?

Does the tree stop giving shade and bearing fruit?

They all are alive!

Don't tell me they don't know love, for they

Are the true givers and masters of Life

Imbued with God, telling us that Love is not to *have*

But to *give,* enjoy, believe, and take part in –

But who am I?

I come from nowhere, I'm just passing by, watching

Your craving for attention, reconciliation, Love

Seeking the essence that surrounds you

Which would permeate you – if you only

Closed your eyes

And opened up your Heart.

Finding Faith

I lost all I have ever won

I cowered in the dark, alone

In pains that I had never known...

Then God came, and said: "Carry on!"

I sailed like a deserted swan

Soulless, mindless, searching for love

God gave me hope, for I was good,

And with God's grace, I carried on

My pools of tears, life woebegone,

Turned into ponds of Love and Faith

My friends praised me for being brave...

I said: God made me carry on –

I am God's creature, He is mine

I am a part of His Design.

Beauty Is All

All I shall ever seek in life
Is Beauty – Beauty is all
That there is to life, and all
I will ever want to know

Books, lectures, degrees – they're just talk
Cold, empty air – nothing there!
No rainbow, bird, flower to smell
Save for the professor's mouth –

And even the prettiest of songs
Pales before a chirping bird!
You increase the volume, and
That is how Beauty ends –

Squashed by loudness, meaningless noise
Silenced by the ignorant
Shredded, wasted on the blind
And trampled by human greed

Still, Beauty is all I seek in life

Beauty is all I want to find

Beauty is all I'll ever need.

The Old Beech Tree

You won't find it in any book
The place is so plain no-one knows
Nor would they care to pause and look
At the burdock and barren rose

There is an old beech by the brook
Crystal-clear water softly flows
Tiny trout no-one cares to hook
And western Zephyr gently blows

The place is hidden in plain sight
Only one person knows its charm
A little girl who at night
Would find there refuge from world's harm

She would run there with dying light
Embrace the tree, grasp his rough arm
And tell him of her pain and freight
Weeping softly till all grew calm –

Silence of the Tree swathed her Heart

And stilled the turmoil in her Soul

She feared the day when they would part

He gave her strength, He made her whole

And the burdock and barren rose

They too were her friends, she could tell

They knew the secrets, joys and woes

Congealed good sprites and magic spells...

There is an old beech by the brook

This old lady remembers well

That scared girl the Tree once took

Under His leafy wings to dwell

Never to leave, never to part

To shield her from the fires of Hell

From where her Journey once did start

Until the end, the final knell –

You'd search in vain a map or chart

The Tree is right here, in her Heart.

Till the Day Is Done

She dances till the day is done

Till her Beloved comes back home

And swathes her Soul in Love and Peace

In the eternal Happiness

Then the morrow arrives too soon

Awakes them from their blessed swoon

Should they lie fallow through the day?

What is this life if not Love's play?

We live for Love, and love yields Love

When I stare at the stars above

I see past lovers joining hands

The harmony God understands

Forever may we live and love

And one day more - then say: "Enough!"

Then, to the stars, forever true!

May lovers greet the day anew!

We'll shine for them from far above

We'll smile and twinkle back our Love.

Beauty

Beauty is not a thing

Beauty is a process, happening

Beauty is harmony in flow

What you can hear and feel

But never know

Beauty is the song that fills the room

With Desire, Hope, and Love

Inspiring Light and Faith

Filling you with insubstantial fuel

That Vital Force

Which makes us go on

And face the adversities of life

Beauty is calm

Yet always on the run

To appear to those who despair

Who wonder if she's still there

For the poor and lonely

Beyond deserted dreams...

As soon as she's in sight

As soon as Hope and Love fill your Heart

As soon as the Muse begins to speak

You'll grasp her hand and whisper:

I love you! Please, don't go...

She's gone

Moving on

Like a clear blue mountain stream...

And you keep sitting and staring

Part Narcissus, part an aimless voyager:

What if I dare enter?

Shall I? Shall I dare?

What is there I haven't seen or known?

Beauty is the rose that pleases you

With intricate pattern of petals

With smells and colors of God

That live forever and everywhere...

Yet, if you pluck it, it turns all blue

And fades away

Beauty is the bird that sings for you

Invisible, somewhere, on a branch

Making love even while he's singing

Singing for love

For love knows but song –

Beauty lies on the leaf that's fallen

Into your lap this afternoon

As you were sitting and musing,

Chased by your Mind –

Beauty is all around

Beauty is kind

If you let her, she will hold your hand

And whisper sweet words into your ear –

Your Heart will understand

But you cannot catch her, make her stay

You have to keep looking and finding

Even as you walk along your way

Making ends meet

Pursuing goals...

Which is easy, in a way, because she's here

She surrounds you everywhere

She waits for you, always a few feet ahead,

To bless the path you walk on

And you'll see her there

If you only lift your head

Straighten your stroll, and

Open up your Heart.

Queen Flower

Many a beautiful flower blooms unseen
On a hill, among the burdocks pining
For sunshine and love, a sumptuous queen
One glance, one touch, to Heaven she's twining

From Heaven she's sent pure pleasure to spread
Joy-filled, joy-giving, but planted to Earth
She feels like an angel with wings of lead
A discarded gem, a misfit from birth

And, once in a while, a passer-by comes
A lover of Nature, beautiful flowers
He smells her, he strokes her, gently he hums...
Softly, she smiles – she has heavenly powers!

He will not pluck her, for he knows too well
You can't own Beauty, it isn't a thing
It is the feeling, the touch, kiss, and smell
Something within you that you yourself bring

That makes the Queen Flower all blossom and shine

At morning, she opens fresh dew to drink

And when the moon comes, her petals decline

Of you she'll dream, and rise up in the pink

No matter your age, you're never apart

For now, forever, she is in your Heart.

Something in Between

Much have I traveled in the realms of Pain

And many miserable states have seen

From North to South, from East to West have been

By Will and Heart have gone – I can't complain

It was my road, my choice, and I was keen

On every step, and pause, and dream, and sight

At every place I lay to spend the night

With Socrates and Jesus, in between

The world of Man and God, where angels sing

O'er human voices from a distant room

And terrors of my days recede to swoon

Until I lose my form and grow a wing...

I stared at the Pacific Sun a-gleam

Casting His arrows straight into my Heart

Bleeding my Pain, as I did at the start...

Much have I traveled, many places seen

But I remain as I have always been:

Part mad, part angel – something in between.

To Melody

What would I be

    Without friends?

Friends like you, Melody

    With open hands

Wearing the Heart on the sleeve

Soothing words, gifts as sweet

    As honeydew and mead –

Hope and Faith and Trust

    With eyes sincere

    And common sense

All that, and more – to share

And when you leave, I know

    You haven't left

You are still there for me

    You know, and care

    And I am here

Knowing, believing, loving

For what else is Friendship

But Trust and Faith and Love:

    A helping hand

A shoulder to cry on

A Soul to confide in

Something beyond and above

Which we can't define

But it is always there

When you rejoice, or despair

When you ask

It answers the call

Does not hesitate

To rush to help and sooth...

I am rich and blessed

To have a friend that's true

I am rich and blessed

To have a Friend like You.

Give Me Your Heart

Give me your Heart, but not your Soul

Give me your thoughts, but not your mind

Give me your time – not all, not all

For I'll want more, and you're too kind

But be not too soft, too quick to yield

Be not too blind to my own charm

I have less grasp on powers I wield

But much more potency to harm

I'll pray each day to remember

It is in giving we receive

And should our Fire turn to embers

I won't reproach, I'll only grieve

But let's be joyful, let's believe

We'll last as long as this stout tree

If we remember Love must breathe

And come and go at Liberty

For parting is but sorrow sweet

When we both know we shall return

And though my Heart may skip a beat

I feel but pleasure when I yearn

And once fulfilled, I'll yearn again

Oh, what great Pleasure in this Pain!

One Is All You Need

What do you seek from life?

Success? A fortune? Fame?

For which one do you strife

Which one reflects your name?

What do you seek from life?

A family, a wife entrenched?

To be admired and liked?

To have your needs all quenched?

Here's what I seek, here's all

I'll ever want or need:

My Love, from Spring to Fall

And Winter too, indeed

When I fade, times turn sour

My Love is here and says

"Do not despair this hour

God tests your Faith, I guess..."

My Love is smart and true

My Love will never leave

And when I'm down and blue

In Love I still Believe

And I am sure you too

Have yours – here, or above

A Love that's just as true

As mine, and just as tough –

Many are forms of love

All roses, none is weed

Many are forms of love

But one is all your need.

I Feel You Everywhere

The doggies laze the day away

The cats play naughty in the house

The birds are chirping as I pray

As silent as a little mouse

A silent observer am I

A tourist in the Beauty Land

Birdies and squirrels catch my eye –

They know me, and I understand

They are here for me, I for them

God placed me here to love and care

Each living creature is a gem

And all we have, we all must share

I kiss the roses on my way

To feed the rowdy alley cats

A hyacinth leans in my way:

Pardon me, Sir, you'd like to pet?

His phallic stare, his smiling eye...

For sure I know what's on his mind!

Naw, just needs water – so do I

And he is modest and refined

All is well in that realm of ours

That you and I together built

The dogs and cats and birds and flowers...

Though we may weep at times, and wilt

For you aren't here to see us all

And I sit in your empty chair

Imbue the Beauty, mark the call –

God telling me to love and share

To open my Soul and my Heart

To close my eyes... then, everywhere

I feel your touch and smell your hair

And I then know we're not apart

I feel your lips on mine, I swear

I smile, rejoice, and kiss the air.

I Have No Fear

I have no fear

The fridge is softly humming on

The flowers in the vase, water fresh

The dogs asleep, the cats – who knows...

I have no fear

I do not lock the doors at night

(Though you, Angel, wouldn't need a key)

The lights are dimmed, I muse and swoon...

I have no fear

Semi-naked, from room to room

I thoughtless stroll, immersed in Me

My past, a cat-toy at my feet –

I have no fear

I sip of wine and live my days

Timelessly, in the outer space

Tranquil, pristine – save for the cat

That paws my past with innocence

Teaching me how to live alone

Without you, among these four walls...

I have no fear.

Without Regrets

There may be something we haven't done –

Sawing wood together

Planting a tree, building a house...?

Yet, we have been through thick and thin

On the ground, in the air

Needing no promises or vows

In the sea we may not have swum

Kicked the ball, thrown a kite...?

Hold on! We did those, I recall

If my memory serves me right

We planted a few trees

You built this house, once we used

A handsaw to cut naughty woods

The sharp old olive tree

Whose branch near poked me in the eye...

If there is something we haven't done

Then I guess it's not worth doing

Or can't be done at all –

So now I'm staring at the sky

Saying Good-Bye to You...

Without regrets, my Love –

For we have had it all.

Aging Beauty

Festering lilies I have never seen

Yet, fading Beauty I know well...

Old Age is no less beautiful and keen

Than fast-stirred-up excited youth can tell

Try fading roses – don't they smell the best!

You need no perfume on your lips...

Only such Love which lasts is truly blessed

For who can trust unweathered, unsailed ships?

Festering lilies I have never seen

I cannot vouch for the Old Master's words...

True Beauty from a puppy you must wean

Supply with love, and faith, and care – in thirds

The last third directs you to never miss

To pass by any rose without a kiss

For youth is a pet longing for a thrill

Growing to Beauty, offering sweet smell

And you will need to cultivate your skill

For Beauty which has aged is sweeter still.

It Happened One Day

We're Soul-to-Soul and Heart-to-Heart

Do not ask me "Where did it start?"

It happened one day, just like that

Planned not by me or you, but God

It came like rain after a drought

When we were tired and so worn out

We could see but a day ahead

And others drove us sad and mad...

And then we met, and struck a chord

Resounding in a sweet accord

For down below, deep in our past

There rest adventures unsurpassed

It's genes of giants tie us in

Our forefathers, each loss and win

That's chartered on the course we've sailed

That's told in tallest of our tales

Stories that sound like fairy tales

Or pitches for outrageous sales –

But only you and I will know

Which ones are true, which for the show

And every word, and every glance

Lead us to share this starry dance

To share with those who are not here

Before we too must disappear...

Meanwhile, we meet, and talk, and love

Split easy joys and moments tough

Reminding others that there's more –

Another ship, another shore

Behind the corner, at the end

Of what we some deem My Last Stand

For that is how we met at first –

Life is a movie unrehearsed

And those who rehearse, to play "tough"

They'll never have true Friend or Love.

Time

Ciphered old dial-handed Time

Chronos, of Earth and Water made

With Einstein's space You intertwine

Give birth to us, then slowly fade...

Intangible and unperceived

Unless we think of Love or Death

Chaos and Air You once conceived

Transforming in our every breath

In silence, the Heart speaks to me

In rhythm ticking on the wall

Uncompromising Destiny

Yet, I refuse to hear Your call!

Midday and midnight pass so fast

Your dial hands play tricks on me

Like spinning wheels, or ship's main mast

Or an unbending, robust tree

They stare at me, always waiting
For my question, a fearful gaze
I am the bird that they're baiting
To fill me with pride and false praise:

"Here you are, my friend, old and wise
Fear not the other side of life!
We're pointing up, to Paradise
To free you from this earthly strife…"

They cast no shadow, yet the blame
Is heavier than what I can bear
I crumble, fall, at Chronos swear
I tear my hair out in despair!

So many things I should have done…
So many places left unseen!
What seconds' worth of distance run
Will never be, and never mean!

I sigh and smile at my advent:

With Life I've had a Grand Romance!

Yonder awaits me my best friend

The Love of my Life begs a dance

I feel his touch, he takes my hand...

Good Bye, All! And thank You, my Lord

for every chance.

Made in the USA
Las Vegas, NV
15 December 2020

13572060R00069